RICK RODGERS

PICNICS AND TAILGATE PARTIES

Surefire recipes and exciting menus for a flawless party!

RICK RODGERS

PICNICS AND TAILGATE PARTIES

Surefire recipes and exciting menus for a flawless party!

ILLUSTRATIONS BY ROBBIN GOURLEY

WARNER ☯ TREASURES™

PUBLISHED BY WARNER BOOKS

A TIME WARNER COMPANY

Text copyright © 1996 by Rick Rodgers
Illustrations copyright © 1996 by Robbin Gourley

Warner Treasures is a trademark of Warner Books, Inc.

Warner Books, Inc.
1271 Avenue of the Americas
New York, NY 10020

 A Time Warner Company

Book design by Robbin Gourley
Printed in Singapore
First Printing: March 1996
10 9 8 7 6 5 4 3 2 1

ISBN: 0-446-91094-5

CONTENTS

INTRODUCTION 7

AN ALFRESCO SUPPER IN THE PARK 17

A TAILGATE PARTY 35

A PICNIC AT THE BEACH 49

INTRODUCTION

W H A T I S I T A B O U T outdoor entertaining that is so allur-ing? Is it the close proximity to Mother Nature, source for the bounty that is served from the picnic basket? Is it the fresh air that piques the appetite, making practically anything we eat taste so much better?

There are many opportunities for parties to be held outdoors, from plain and simple to fancy and elegant. As a child of suburban California in the fifties, I saw outdoor meals as a way of life. From the first warm days of April until a chill was in the air in October (or later), many of the family's dinners were cooked on our trusty kettle grill and served at the redwood table in our backyard. Dessert was as simple as walking over to the apricot or peach tree, reaching up, and picking a ripe fruit. Weekend outings at the park or beach meant packing a cooler of favorite sandwiches and salads. When autumn weather finally arrived, the picnics became hearty tailgate parties held in the parking lot of the high school, as my friends and their families prepared to cheer on the team. November was usually mild, and although it was too cold to eat on the patio, many families prepared the Thanksgiving turkey on the grill, bringing the outdoor flavors inside to the dining room. Even in the dead of winter, when we gathered for caroling in the neighborhood, we would sing with thermoses of hot cider and pockets full of brownies.

The origin of the word *picnic* is shrouded in mystery. (I visualize its origins as the fragrant haze of smoke rising from a charcoal-burning grill.) English-speaking gourmets may assume that the phrase comes from the act of "picking" at the viands offered at an outdoor meal. The first written incidence of the word, however, occurred in French—*pique-nique*—and its literal meaning has nothing to do with food. A *pique* is a pike or staff (vaguely associated with the connotation to pique one's interest or appetite). *Nique* has no exact translation, but when used in certain idioms (*faire la nique à la fortune,* or "to despise riches") has a negative implication. Perhaps its rhyming sound had some connection with a certain food or meal, but no one knows for sure. Originally it referred to a meal where each guest contributed a dish, like today's potluck supper. How this meal traveled outdoors is anyone's guess.

Outdoor eating, of course, has been around ever since Eve and the apple in the garden (and she and Adam certainly ate before that unfortunate incident, too). But it was the French court of the 1700s that made this type of entertaining fashionable. As an antidote to the baroque intrigues of court politics, artificial depictions of peasant life, called pastorals, were staged by the courtiers. Of course, peasants ate outdoors a lot, and the gentlemen and ladies would dress up as shepherds and milkmaids at these affairs and have their meals served *en plein air*. After the Revolution, class distinctions were virtually erased in France, so the fashion of outdoor dining was extinguished.

It was up to the British to revive the custom, and again class distinctions set the pace. As the middle class developed and became richer, excursions out of the urban, moneymaking centers became stylish (and necessary to breathe some fresh air). The more food and provisions the host could afford to carry to the country illustrated his wealth—showing off for the Joneses was partly the purpose for all the fuss. Not for nothing do many of us equate fancy outdoor meals with the English hunt picnic, with its fine china and silver trundled to a sylvan spot and set out on a thick Scottish plaid blanket. Now we have simple outdoor parties because they are enjoyable.

With a little planning, outdoor entertaining can be not only fun but easy. When planning a menu, I pick foods that I know will transport easily. (Backyard entertaining is a different situation; this book addresses food that will be carried a distance to a site.) For example, for dessert, brownies (which are firm and don't crumble) win over a frosted layer cake (whose frosting will get messed up during travel). Practically every picnic dish should be made a day ahead of time, waiting to be packed the next morning, sidestepping any last-minute fussing. Therefore, I make dishes that improve with marinating or can be made well ahead without getting stale or soggy. (One tip—potato and pasta salads soak up their dressing and need to be reseasoned before serving, so I always bring some extra dressing, salt, and pepper.) The menus I suggest here will make it to the park, beach, or stadium in one piece. But certain tools and equipment will smooth the way.

First on your list is a sturdy **cooler.** I have a number of thick, inexpensive Styrofoam coolers in various sizes. You may want to purchase a top-notch metal or plastic model that will last years. I also like the light, soft thermal fabric coolers, their shoulder straps making them very easy to carry. If you are a serious picnic or tailgate party giver, buy both a large-size cooler to carry foods and a smaller one to act as a beverage server. This way, the food will not lose its chill having to share cooler space with the sodas, where the lid is constantly opened by thirsty picnickers. Thermal coolers will also hold hot foods at serving temperature (see page 38 for tips on how to transport hot foods).

My freezer always holds a stash of **thermal gel-packs** ("blue ice") to keep the food ice cold. These wonders of technology are much more efficient than ice cubes, which always seem to melt and get into the food, no matter how tightly wrapped. If you require ice cubes to put in beverages, you can forgo the thermal packs but make sure the inside of the cooler is well washed. If you have any doubts, place the ice cubes in a small plastic garbage bag and close it tightly.

Covered containers come in all shapes and sizes, but I find the rectangular ones fit most efficiently into coolers. Round styles, which often can double as servers, leave too much wasted space. (Who said serving bowls have to be round?) Store-and-serve containers have another advantage: they are light and easy to carry.

Picnic baskets give a tone of authenticity to the proceedings, but I find that the old-fashioned wicker ones aren't always practical. They are fine for carrying plates and utensils, but they don't hold much food and usually aren't thermal. You can purchase a gorgeously fitted picnic hamper with real china and silver, but before you do, think about who in your group is going to be strong enough to lug it. Look for lightweight baskets with well-made plastic plates and utensils.

Unless you are bringing along the butler to carry the china, purchase sturdy **plastic or paper plates,** now available in an array of colors and designs. But, choose your plates for their strength, not their visual appeal, since the only thing worse than ants at a picnic is a dripping, flimsy plate of food. **Plastic utensils** are a must. I used to bring my inexpensive flatware along, but no matter how hard I would try, I always left a piece behind. Glassware gives you a range of choices. If I am serving a homemade beverage, like lemonade or sangria, I bring see-through plastic glasses because the beverages seem to taste better when you can see them through the glass. Otherwise, I use hot/cold paper cups, since I also often serve hot beverages and I don't want to supply two kinds of cups. Use **paper napkins** unless you are super-organized—I always leave my household cloth napkins behind too, to keep my lost flatware company! Don't forget to bring along a **large plastic garbage bag** or two for disposing of the plates and utensils (unless they are strong enough to rinse off and reuse) and other trash. When you get to your location, scope out the nearest water source for rinsing the containers before you repack and leave.

Outdoor meals often, but not always, entail cooking outdoors. Many parks have stationary grills, but unless you get there at the crack of dawn to stake a claim, they are often all taken by the time you arrive, especially during busy holiday weekends. It is much smarter to bring your own grill. I have two Weber **kettle grills**—the standard 22-inch model and a smaller portable one. It is easier than you think to pull the legs out of the large model and put the whole thing in the car trunk (you just slip the legs back into their holes when you get to the picnic). The large grill allows you to grill food for a number of guests. The smaller grill can cook main courses for a group of four, or can be brought along to cook appetizers only. If you bring a grill along, choose a safe location for maintaining the fire, and be sure to have a bucket of water or water source nearby. To dispose of the coals, dump them out of the grill onto a spot that you have already made wet, then douse them until you are sure they are dead. I was witness to a bad accident once where the coals were buried in sand, then someone stepped on the spot in bare feet, so please follow my advice. Rinse out the grill to cool down before you leave. Small tabletop propane gas grills are available, but I much prefer the flavor of charcoal-grilled foods. For tailgate parties, I sometimes reheat food on a **propane-fueled portable burner** called a *cassette feu*.

But, as I said earlier, anything tastes better when cooked outdoors!

SUPPLIES CHECKLIST

Here's a checklist that you may want to use for your next outdoor party. Bring a copy of it with you to the site, so you can check things off as you repack them. That way you won't leave anything behind.

- ☐ Food—make a menu and check things off as you pack them; don't forget salad dressing for reseasoning pre-made salads
- ☐ Frozen thermal gel-packs—don't forget to put them in the freezer the night before
- ☐ Ice cubes, if using—make plenty the night before, or purchase
- ☐ Plates
- ☐ Forks, knives, spoons
- ☐ Plastic glasses and paper cups
- ☐ Serving dishes
- ☐ Serving utensils
- ☐ Tablecloth and/or picnic blanket
- ☐ Napkins
- ☐ Salt and pepper
- ☐ Wine opener, bottle opener, can opener
- ☐ Serrated knife and small cutting board—very handy, even if you've precut everything
- ☐ A wet sponge in a plastic bag for easy cleanup

- [ ] Premoistened hand towelettes—for cleaning hands during preparation and after meals
- [ ] Paper towels
- [ ] Plastic wrap for leftovers
- [ ] Plastic garbage bags
- [ ] Cushions or foldable chairs
- [ ] Portable radio, cassette, or CD player with tapes or CDs—check batteries
- [ ] Sunscreen
- [ ] Insect repellent
- [ ] First-aid kit—for cut fingers or burns
- [ ] Charcoal grill
- [ ] Charcoal—be sure to have enough
- [ ] Matches
- [ ] Kindling for grill (if at beach) or charcoal lighter

AN ALFRESCO SUPPER IN THE PARK

MEDITERRANEAN RICOTTA SPREAD

TORTA RUSTICA

MARINATED MUSHROOMS AND ARTICHOKE HEARTS

WHITE BEANS WITH SUN-DRIED TOMATO PESTO

Summertime Sangria

CHOCOLATE-HAZELNUT BISCOTTI

Iced Tea or Coffee

For 8 to 10 people

LIVING AS I DO IN the New York City area, I could go to a different outdoor cultural event every night of the summer, often without paying a cent. The phone rings every few days with a call from a friend. Shall we go to see Shakespeare in the park? Did you hear that they're giving *La Traviata* tomorrow night at the bandshell? How would you like to go two-step dancing in Lincoln Center plaza next week? I'm sure you have many such opportunities in your community, from a band concert in the town square to a theatrical production in an amphitheater. Invariably I accept, and they ask, "Wouldn't you like to put together something for us to eat?" I sure would!

My style is to bring delicious food that is easy to transport, serve, and eat. Some fellow culture lovers come to the event loaded down with portable tables, lace tablecloths, expensive china and crystal, even candelabras (I kid you not!). Give me a blanket and a good thermal carrier, and I'm happy. All of the food is made a day or two ahead. Even if I come home at 5 P.M., it's simply a matter of packing the cooler. (Yes, if I got to Central Park as late as 6 P.M., I could be miles from the stage. Usually one member of the group volunteers to secure a spot early in the afternoon. I hope life is less complicated where you live.)

Because much of my favorite vocal music is Italian opera, and I find myself attending Verdi or Puccini works often, a Mediterranean-inspired supper seems appropriate. My menu is a bit more festive than the usual picnic fare (just in case the people with the china and silver look over to my blanket to see what a food writer makes for his friends at a picnic). Usually all of the guests are adults, so I don't have to consider the taste preferences of children. I love to serve dips at my outdoor parties—they're informal, tasty, and fun. I start with a Mediterranean Ricotta Spread to serve with crackers or baguette slices. Torta Rustica is a very special main course. It takes a bit of time to make (I use frozen puff pastry to speed up the preparation), but it looks and tastes great, so you will be rewarded for your trouble. Two marinated salads, White Beans with Sun-Dried Tomato Pesto and Marinated Mushrooms and Artichoke Hearts, round out the supper. Rather than serve wine from a bottle, I make a special beverage, Summertime Sangria, with summer-ripe peaches and raspberries. For dessert, there are Chocolate-Hazelnut Biscotti, mouthwatering cookies that are pretty difficult to crush during transport. They can be dipped into the sangria—or iced coffee, if you've brought along a second thermos—but even without dunking, they are a fitting finale.

PREPARATION TIMETABLE

Up to 1 week ahead:

⋆ Bake Chocolate-Hazelnut Biscotti; store in an airtight container at room temperature.

Up to 5 days ahead:

⋆ Make Marinated Mushroom and Artichoke Hearts salad; cover and refrigerate.

Up to 2 days ahead:

⋆ Make Mediterranean Ricotta Spread; cover and refrigerate.

⋆ Make Torta Rustica; cover and refrigerate.

⋆ Make White Bean salad; cover and refrigerate.

Up to 1 day ahead:

⋆ Make Summertime Sangria; cover and refrigerate.

⋆ Make beverage for iced coffee or tea; cool, cover and refrigerate.

MEDITERRANEAN RICOTTA SPREAD

Makes 2 ¼ cups

When spread on crackers or baguette slices, this surefire blend of ricotta, sun-dried tomatoes, garlic, and basil is reminiscent of everyone's favorite, pizza. If the meal is a picnic where everyone is spread out on a blanket, put the spread and crackers on two platters and place them at opposite ends of the blanket so the guests can serve themselves without too much reaching.

1 (15-ounce) container ricotta cheese
½ cup (3 ounces) sun-dried tomatoes in oil, drained and chopped
3 tablespoons chopped fresh basil
1 garlic clove, crushed through a press
⅛ teaspoon crushed hot red pepper flakes
Salt, to taste
Crackers or baguette slices, for serving

1. In a medium bowl, combine ricotta, sun-dried tomatoes, basil, garlic, and red pepper flakes. Season with salt to taste. *The spread can be prepared up to 2 days ahead, covered, and refrigerated.*

2. Place bowl on a serving platter and serve with a knife for spreading on crackers.

TORTA RUSTICA

Makes 8 to 10 servings

There are few picnic main courses more attractive than this multilayered, many-colored torta rustica. It should be made ahead and chilled for easy slicing, but bring it to room temperature before serving.

Spinach Layer

2 tablespoons olive oil
1 small red onion, chopped
2 garlic cloves, minced
2 (10-ounce) packages frozen chopped spinach, thawed, squeezed in batches to remove excess moisture
1 teaspoon dried basil
¼ teaspoon salt
⅛ teaspoon freshly ground pepper

Egg Layer

12 large eggs
½ teaspoon salt
⅛ teaspoon freshly ground pepper
2 tablespoons olive oil, divided

1 (17¼-ounce) package prepared puff pastry sheets, thawed
1 large egg white, beaten until foamy
½ cup (2 ounces) freshly grated Parmesan cheese
8 ounces sliced Swiss cheese
8 ounces sliced smoked ham or smoked turkey
2 (7½-ounce) jars marinated roasted red peppers, rinsed, drained, and patted dry
1 large egg yolk, beaten with 1 tablespoon milk, for glazing

1. Make the spinach layer: In a large skillet, heat oil over medium heat. Add onion and cook until translucent, about 5 minutes. Add garlic and stir for 1 minute. Add spinach, basil, salt, and pepper. Cook, stirring constantly, until moisture evaporates from spinach and spinach begins to stick slightly to skillet, about 3 minutes. Transfer to a medium bowl and cool completely.

2. Make the egg layer: In a large bowl, whisk eggs, salt, and pepper until well combined. In a medium skillet, preferably nonstick, heat 1 tablespoon oil over medium heat. Add half of the egg mixture and cook, stirring often, until eggs are soft-set, about 1½ minutes. Transfer to another medium bowl. Repeat procedure with remaining oil and eggs. Set aside to cool completely.

3. Position a rack in center of oven, and place a baking sheet on the rack. (The baking sheet is important, as it helps set the bottom crust and catches any dripping butter from the cooking pastry.) Preheat oven to 425°F. Lightly butter the inside of a 9-inch round springform pan.

Tightly wrap bottom of pan with a double thickness of aluminum foil.

4. On a lightly floured work surface, roll out one sheet of puff pastry to ⅛-inch thickness. Carefully transfer pastry to prepared pan, pressing dough against sides of pan and let-

ting excess pastry hang over edges. Brush inside of dough lightly with some of the beaten egg white.

5. Sprinkle dough with ¼ cup of Parmesan cheese, then top with half of the sliced Swiss cheese. Layer with one-half smoked ham or turkey, then top with half of the peppers. Spread with half of spinach mixture, then half of the beaten eggs. Repeat with remaining spinach, then eggs. Follow with layers of remaining peppers, ham or turkey, Swiss cheese, then Parmesan cheese.

6. Roll out remaining sheet of pastry to ⅛-inch thickness. Center the pastry on top of filling. Cut a ⁵⁄₁₆-inch-wide hole out of the center of the pastry to allow steam to escape. Press dough together firmly to seal. With a sharp knife or scissors, trim away excess dough at pan's edge,

leaving ½-inch-wide border of dough. (If desired, reserve pastry trimmings to cut into decorations.) Roll up dough into a thick rope, and pinch and flute with fingers. Brush top lightly with some of the yolk glaze. If using, place pastry decorations on top, and brush decorations lightly with glaze.

7. Place springform pan on preheated baking sheet in oven. Bake for 10 minutes. Reduce heat to 325°F. and continue baking until golden brown, 50 minutes to 1 hour. Cool completely in pan on a wire cake rack. *The torta can be prepared up to 2 days ahead, cooled, covered tightly with foil, and refrigerated.*

8. Remove sides of pan. Use a serrated knife to cut into wedges and serve at room temperature.

MARINATED MUSHROOMS AND ARTICHOKE HEARTS

Makes 8 to 10 servings

I love these tangy vegetables, which are zippy enough to be called pickles but substantially mellowed by olive oil to serve as a chunky salad. Buy mushrooms that are all the same size, no bigger than 1 inch across, so they will cook evenly.

2½ cups water
2 cups white or red wine vinegar
1 teaspoon dried tarragon
2 bay leaves
2 garlic cloves, crushed
½ teaspoon salt
¼ teaspoon crushed hot red pepper flakes
20 ounces medium whole fresh mushrooms
2 (9-ounce) packages frozen artichoke hearts, thawed
½ cup extra-virgin olive oil
2 tablespoons chopped fresh parsley

1. In a large saucepan, combine water, vinegar, tarragon, bay leaves, garlic, salt, and red pepper flakes. Bring to a simmer over medium heat. Add mushrooms. Reduce heat to low and simmer for 15 minutes.

2. Add artichoke hearts and continue cooking for 5 minutes. Remove from heat and let stand for 10 minutes. Drain well. Transfer to a large bowl. Add oil and toss well. Cool completely. Cover and refrigerate for at least overnight. *The vegetables can be prepared up to 5 days ahead, covered, and refrigerated.*

3. Remove from refrigerator at least 1 hour ahead. Sprinkle with parsley and toss well. Serve the salad at room temperature.

WHITE BEANS WITH SUN-DRIED TOMATO PESTO

Makes 8 to 12 servings

Versatile, firm, and meaty cannellini beans (also called white kidney beans) are a chameleon of the Mediterranean kitchen, easily transformed by various seasonings like this tasty dressing. Try to start with dried beans, but in a pinch you can substitute six (15-ounce) cans of beans, drained and rinsed.

1 pound dried cannellini (white kidney) beans, rinsed and picked over for stones
1 medium yellow onion, peeled and left whole
2 bay leaves
2 teaspoons plus ¾ teaspoon salt
3 ounces loose-packed sun-dried tomatoes (see Note)
3 tablespoons red wine vinegar

1 garlic clove, crushed
¼ teaspoon crushed hot red pepper flakes
¾ cup olive oil
2 tablespoons chopped fresh sage, or 2 teaspoons dried
1 pound ripe plum tomatoes, cut into ½-inch pieces
1 small red onion, chopped

1. The day before serving, soak the beans: In a large bowl, place beans and add enough cold water to cover beans by 2 inches. Let stand at room temperature overnight. (Do not use quick-soak methods to rehydrate cannellini beans—the beans tend to fall apart during cooking.)

2. Drain the beans. Place in a large saucepan and add enough fresh water to cover by 2 inches. Add onion and bay leaves. Bring to a boil over high

heat. Reduce heat to low and simmer for 15 minutes. Add 2 teaspoons of the salt, and continue simmering until beans are tender, about 25 minutes. (The exact cooking time depends on age and dryness of beans.) Drain again and place in a large bowl.

3. Meanwhile, in a small bowl, place sun-dried tomatoes and add enough boiling water to cover. Let stand until softened, from 3 to 30 minutes depending on dryness of tomatoes. Drain well and transfer to a food processor fitted with the metal blade or a blender.

4. Add the vinegar, garlic, remaining ¾ teaspoon salt, and red pepper flakes and process until finely chopped. With the machine running, gradually add olive oil in a stream. Transfer to a small bowl and stir in sage. *The sun-dried tomato pesto can be prepared up to 1 day ahead, covered, and refrigerated.*

5. Add the pesto, plum tomatoes, and red onion to the beans and toss well. Cover and refrigerate for at least 2 hours to allow the flavors to blend. *The salad can be prepared up to 2 days ahead, covered, and refrigerated.* Serve salad at room temperature.

Note: Sun-dried tomatoes are different, depending on where they were processed. Some have been treated with sulphur dioxide, so their color is brighter with a chewy texture. These will take only a few minutes of soaking until rehydrated. The darker, tougher sun-dried tomatoes have no sulphur, and will take longer to soak. To my taste, I prefer the second variety.

SUMMERTIME SANGRIA

Makes 3 quarts

Sangrias often have oranges and apples in them, making them easy to serve year-round. But my favorite sangria, a felicitous blend of raspberries, peaches, Grand Marnier, and red wine, should be made at the height of summer. One afternoon, my friend Rose Levy Beranbaum and I concocted this to celebrate a few of our mutually favorite flavors. Here's to you, Rose.

4 large ripe peaches, unpeeled, pitted and
    cut into ½-inch pieces
1 pint fresh raspberries
½ cup orange-flavored liqueur, such as
    Grand Marnier, or orange juice
¼ cup sugar (increase to ½ cup if using
    orange juice)
2 (750 ml) bottles light, dry red wine, such
    as Rioja or Beaujolais, well chilled

1. The day before serving, combine peaches, raspberries, Grand Marnier, and sugar in a medium bowl. Cover tightly and refrigerate until fruit gives off juices, at least 6 hours or overnight.

2. Stir in red wine. Transfer to a thermos to transport. Serve chilled, over ice, giving each person some of the soaked fruit in his or her glass.

CHOCOLATE-HAZELNUT BISCOTTI

Makes about 28 biscotti

Biscotti, those crisp Italian cookies that have become so popular in the last few years, are often so hard that they must be dipped first in coffee, tea, or sweet wine in order to be safely nibbled. My version is crunchy without being dangerous to dental work—if you want to dunk, go ahead, but I like them *au naturel*.

2 ounces (½ cup) hazelnuts
8 tablespoons (1 stick) unsalted butter, at room temperature
1 cup sugar
Grated zest of 1 large orange
2 large eggs
1 teaspoon vanilla extract
2 cups plus 2 tablespoons all-purpose flour
1 teaspoon baking powder
¼ teaspoon salt
½ cup (3 ounces) mini-chocolate chips

1. Position racks in top third and center of oven and preheat to 350°F. Spread hazelnuts on a baking sheet and bake in top third of oven until skins are cracked, about 10 minutes. Place nuts in a clean kitchen towel and rub together to remove as much skin as possible. Cool nuts, then chop coarsely.

2. In a large bowl, using a handheld electric mixer set at high speed, beat

butter, sugar, and orange zest until very light in color and texture, about 2 minutes. One at a time, beat in eggs, then vanilla.

3. Sift flour, baking powder, and salt together onto a piece of waxed paper. With mixer on low speed, gradually beat in flour mixture just until a smooth dough forms. Using a wooden spoon, stir in chocolate chips and chopped hazelnuts.

4. Divide dough in half. Using lightly floured hands on a floured work surface, form dough into two 10-by-

2-inch rectangular logs. Place logs on ungreased baking sheet, at least 2 inches apart. Bake until logs are set and golden brown, about 30 minutes. Remove from oven and let cool on baking sheet for 20 minutes.

5. Using a serrated knife and a sawing motion, carefully cut logs into diagonal slices about ½ inch wide. Place slices on ungreased baking sheets. Bake on top and center racks of oven until undersides are lightly browned, about 8 minutes. Turn biscotti over, switch position of baking sheets from top to bottom, and continue baking until lightly browned on the other side, about 8 minutes longer. Cool completely on baking sheets. *The biscotti can be prepared up to 1 week ahead, cooled, and tightly covered in an airtight container at room temperature.*

A TAILGATE PARTY

ASSORTED CHEESES, APPLES, AND PRETZELS*

PORK AND RED PEPPER CAZUELA

SPANISH POTATO SALAD WITH SHERRY VINAIGRETTE

CALABASITAS SALAD

FRESHLY BAKED FRENCH OR ITALIAN BREAD*

Mulled Cider Tea

Rioja or Beaujolais Wine

PEAR AND WALNUT SPICE CAKE

For 8 people

*Recipe not included

I WAS TEMPTED TO CALL this "A Tailgate Party at the Stadium," but I realized that there are many opportunities to serve this kind of a warming, hearty meal at events other than football games. A day at the racetrack, a ballooning exhibit, an apple-picking party at a nearby farm, sledding, cross-country skiing, or an ice-skating excursion—all of these are good reasons to pack up the back of the station wagon with good food and drink.

A station wagon is not a necessary part of a tailgate party, although I have been known to rent one because it does make things easier. It is also possible to bring a card table with a tablecloth to set up the food. Ask your friends to bring another one along in their car, too.

Winning tailgate parties provide hot food to heat the insides and fuel the spirits for activities ahead. Since station wagons don't come with four-burner stoves and ovens, I don't expect the entire meal to be hot. But it isn't too much trouble to serve a hot main dish and a steaming thermos-packed beverage. In this menu, a Spanish specialty, Pork and Red Pepper Cazuela, is the centerpiece of the meal. For best flavor, I always make my stews a day ahead, cool, refrigerate, and reheat the next day. There are many ways to transport a hot stew to a site. One way is to reheat the stew at home in an attractive, heavy pot that can be used for serving. (I use an enameled Le Creuset Dutch oven.) Wrap the pot with layers of newspapers and tape it shut with masking tape. The newspaper will insulate the pot and keep it hot for a couple of hours. You can also line the bottom of your cooler (coolers will keep things warm, too) with a heavy thickness of newspaper to protect it from coming in contact with the pot, and transport the stew in the cooler. My preferred method is to transport the refrigerated stew in the serving pot, and reheat it on a propane-fueled burner (*cassette feu*). You can also use a small charcoal or propane tabletop grill for reheating.

With the extra effort needed to reheat the main course, I keep the appetizers simple. Usually I stop off at my neighborhood farmer's market and purchase a farm-made cheddar, two or three kinds of crisp apples, and big, crunchy handmade pretzels. Look around your area for the equivalents—I bet your natural foods store has great organic fruit and some "real" pretzels, and maybe even cheese that hasn't been artificially colored and flavored. I rarely serve green salads at outdoor meals, as the greens will usually stand for a while, and get soggy in the dressing. Marinated salads are much more successful, so this meal is served with Spanish Potato Salad with Sherry Vinaigrette (an unusual variation on a dish that is considered a must at an outdoor meal by many folks) and Calabasitas Salad, a mélange of chunky vegetables in a lime dressing. Sipping Mulled Cider Tea will keep away the chill, and I serve a light red wine like Rioja or Beaujolais for those who wish stronger fortification. A moist Pear and Walnut Spice Cake can be eaten out of hand for the perfect casual dessert.

PREPARATION TIMETABLE

Up to 5 days ahead:
* Purchase pretzels, cheese, and apples.

Up to 3 days ahead:
* Make Pear and Walnut Spice Cake; cool, cover with plastic wrap and store at room temperature.

Up to 2 days ahead:
* Make Pork and Red Pepper Cazuela; cool, cover and refrigerate.

Up to 1 day ahead:
* Make Spanish Potato Salad; cover and refrigerate.
* Make Calabasitas Salad; cover and refrigerate.

Just before leaving:
* Make Mulled Cider Tea; transfer to thermos.
* Reheat Cazuela, if chilled (or reheat at site on butane burner or charcoal grill).

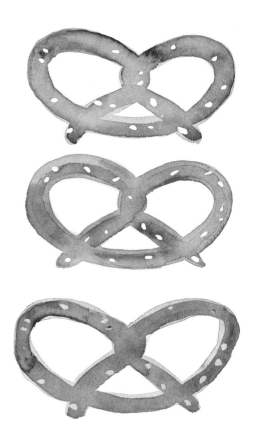

PORK AND RED PEPPER CAZUELA

Makes 8 servings

This stew, rich with the flavors of Spain, improves in flavor if allowed to stand overnight, making it the perfect centerpiece for a tailgate picnic. Pork shoulder (the market may call it *cala* or *pernil* if near a Hispanic community) makes the best stew, as it takes long simmering and soaks up the sauce's flavors as it cooks. Purchase a six-pound pork shoulder, trimming away all of the rind and as much fat as possible. Cut the meat off the bone in 1½-inch chunks to get four pounds of boned meat for the stew. Use boneless pork loin as an alternative, but it is much more expensive and tender—do not simmer for longer than 45 minutes, or it may dry out. The green olives stirred into the stew at the end are an authentic addition, but if you aren't an olive aficionado, leave them out.

2 tablespoons plus 3 tablespoons olive oil, plus more as needed

3 medium onions, cut into ¼-inch-thick half-moons

3 medium red bell peppers, seeded and cut into ½-inch-wide strips

4 garlic cloves, minced

½ cup all-purpose flour

1 teaspoon salt, divided

½ teaspoon freshly ground pepper, divided

4 pounds boneless pork shoulder, cut into 1-inch cubes

1 tablespoon sweet paprika

1 tablespoon dried oregano

1 (16-ounce) can peeled tomatoes in juice, drained and coarsely chopped

1 cup chicken stock, preferably homemade, or use reduced-sodium canned broth

1 cup dry sherry

2 cups pimiento-stuffed green olives, rinsed and drained (optional)

1. In a large, heavy-bottomed pot, heat 2 tablespoons of oil over medium heat. Add the onions, red peppers, and garlic and cover. Cook, stirring often, until the vegetables are softened, about 5 minutes. Transfer to a bowl and set aside.

2. In a medium bowl, combine flour, ½ teaspoon of the salt, and ¼ teaspoon pepper. Transfer 2 tablespoons to a small bowl and set aside.

3. Add the remaining 3 tablespoons of oil to the pot and increase the heat to medium-high. Dredge about one-third of pork in flour mixture, shaking off excess flour. Add to pot without crowding and cook, turning occasionally, until pork is browned on all sides, about 6 minutes. With a slotted spoon, transfer pork to a large bowl. Repeat with remaining pork and flour mixture,

adding more oil to pot as needed. Return browned pork with juices and vegetables to the pot. Add paprika, oregano, the remaining salt and pepper, and stir well. Stir in tomatoes, stock, and sherry. Bring to a simmer, stirring up browned bits on bottom of pot. Reduce heat to low, cover, and simmer until pork is tender, about 2 hours.

4. Add 1 cup of pot liquid to reserved flour and whisk until smooth. Return to pot and, if desired, stir in olives. Cook until sauce is thickened, about 5 minutes. Cool until tepid. Cover and refrigerate for at least 8 hours before serving. *The stew can be prepared up to 2 days ahead, covered, and refrigerated. Reheat gently, stirring often, over medium-low heat until reheated.* Serve hot.

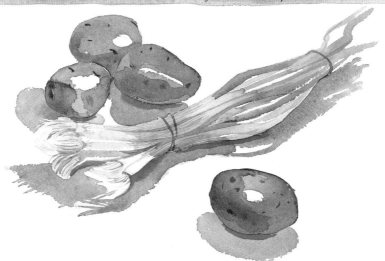

SPANISH POTATO SALAD WITH SHERRY VINAIGRETTE

Makes 8 servings

Sherry vinegar, made just like wine vinegar but from Spanish sherry, is an excellent addition to your pantry. Available at specialty grocers and many supermarkets, it is mellower than most vinegars and adds an elusive flavor to vinaigrettes.

3 pounds medium red-skinned potatoes, well scrubbed
2 large hard-boiled eggs, peeled and sliced
6 scallions, chopped
1 cup black Mediterranean olives, pitted and coarsely chopped (optional)
¼ cup sherry vinegar
½ teaspoon salt
¼ teaspoon freshly ground pepper
¾ cup olive oil
¼ cup chopped fresh parsley

1. In a large pot of boiling, lightly salted water, cook potatoes until just tender when pierced with the tip of a sharp knife, about 25 minutes. Drain and rinse under cold running water until cool enough to handle. Slice into ½-inch-thick rounds and place in a large bowl. Add hard-boiled eggs, scallions, and olives. Toss well.

2. In a medium bowl, whisk vinegar, salt, and pepper. Gradually whisk in oil. Drizzle over salad and toss well. Cover tightly and refrigerate for at least 4 hours. *The salad can be prepared up to 1 day ahead, covered, and refrigerated.*

3. When ready to serve, add parsley and toss well. Taste, and reseason with additional salt and pepper as needed. Serve chilled or at room temperature.

CALABASITAS SALAD

Makes 8 servings

Calabasitas is a popular Mexican vegetable dish of sautéed zucchini and onions with corn and cheese. I have taken these ingredients and turned them into a salad, where the zucchini gets a piquant pickled flavor from the lime vinaigrette. Soaking the red onion in vinegar is an old trick that reduces the onion's bite.

1 medium red onion, finely chopped

½ cup red wine vinegar

4 medium zucchini (about 1 pound, 9 ounces), well scrubbed, trimmed, and cut into ½-inch-thick half-moons

8 ounces Monterey jack cheese, cut into ½-inch cubes

1 pint cherry tomatoes, halved

1 cup fresh or defrosted corn kernels

⅓ cup chopped fresh cilantro

¼ cup lime juice

1 garlic clove, minced

1 fresh hot green chile pepper (such as jalapeño), seeded and minced

½ teaspoon sugar

½ teaspoon salt

¾ cup olive oil

1. In a medium bowl, combine red onion and vinegar. Let stand for 30 minutes. Drain, discarding vinegar.

2. Meanwhile, bring a medium saucepan of lightly salted water to a boil over high heat. Add zucchini and cook until crisp-tender, about 1 minute (water does not have to return to a boil). Drain, rinse under cold water, and drain again. Transfer to a large bowl and add drained onion, cheese, cherry tomatoes, corn, and cilantro.

3. In a medium bowl, whisk lime juice, garlic, chile pepper, sugar, and salt. Gradually whisk in olive oil. Pour dressing over salad and toss. Cover and refrigerate for at least 2 hours for flavors to blend. *The salad can be made up to 1 day ahead, covered, and refrigerated.* Serve at room temperature.

MULLED CIDER TEA

Makes 2 quarts

A warming drink is always welcome at a tailgate party. Use unfiltered apple cider for the best flavor.

1 quart apple cider
½ cup honey
3 (3-inch) cinnamon sticks
12 whole cloves
1 quart boiling water
4 bags orange pekoe tea

1. In a medium saucepan, bring apple cider, honey, cinnamon, and cloves slowly to a simmer over low heat, stirring often to dissolve honey.

2. Meanwhile, in a large bowl, pour boiling water over tea bags. Cover and let stand for 5 minutes. Strain in cider mixture and stir well. Remove tea bags.

3. To transport, pour into a large preheated thermos. Serve hot.

PEAR AND WALNUT SPICE CAKE

Makes 10 to 12 servings

Italian cooks often use olive oil in their desserts, but choose a mild-flavored, golden-hued variety and not extra-virgin, which would be too rich and "olive-y." Cornmeal adds another Mediterranean touch as well as crunch. This moist cake travels well, especially when carried in the same pan as it was baked in. Choose firm Bosc pears for this cake, as other pear varieties like Anjou or Comice may be too juicy and thin out the batter. Make it one day ahead for the best flavor and texture.

2 cups all-purpose flour

½ cup fine yellow cornmeal, preferably stone-ground

1 teaspoon ground cinnamon

1 teaspoon baking soda

½ teaspoon salt

¼ teaspoon grated nutmeg

3 large eggs, at room temperature

2 cups sugar

1 cup olive oil

1 teaspoon vanilla extract

3 ripe-firm, medium Bosc pears, peeled, cored, and cut into ½-inch pieces (about 4 cups)

1 cup coarsely chopped walnuts

1. Preheat oven to 350°F. Butter and flour a 10-inch fluted tube pan, shaking out excess flour.

2. Sift flour, cornmeal, cinnamon, baking soda, salt, and nutmeg onto a piece of waxed paper.

3. In a large bowl, using a handheld electric mixer set at high speed, beat eggs and sugar until combined. Add oil and vanilla and beat until thick and light colored, about 2 minutes. Using a wooden spoon, stir in flour mixture, just until smooth. The batter will be very thick. Stir in pears and walnuts. Transfer to prepared pan, and smooth top.

4. Bake until a toothpick inserted in cake comes out clean, about 60 minutes. Cool in the pan for 10 minutes. Invert onto a wire cake rack, remove mold, and cool completely. The cake improves in flavor if allowed to age overnight, wrapped in plastic and stored at room temperature. *The cake can be prepared up to 3 days ahead, cooled, covered tightly with plastic wrap, and stored at room temperature.*

A PICNIC AT THE BEACH

FRESH SUMMER FRUITS WITH SPIKED YOGURT DIP

GRILLED CHICKEN IN HERB MARINADE

CABBAGE AND SHRIMP SLAW

ORZO SALAD PISTOU

Handmade Lemon-Limeade

BLONDIES WITH WHITE CHOCOLATE CHIPS
AND RASPBERRIES

For 8 people

"SUMMER AFTERNOON ... to me those have always been the two most beautiful words in the English language." This evocative comment is attributed to Henry James, according to Edith Wharton. For me, thoughts of summertime just don't create images of hammocks and baseball. My mind conjures up the feel of a cool glass of lemonade in my hand, the taste of sweet brownies, and the sound of chicken sizzling on the grill.

The quintessential summer picnic is spent by the sea, when the July sun warms the skin and the sea air awakens the appetite. It can also be said that grilling is the summer cooking method of choice. So that I don't have to worry about finding a free stationary grill at popular beaches, I always bring one along. (See pages 12–13 for information on different kinds of grills.)

I serve a selection of summer fruits at their peak with a Spiked

Yogurt Dip (flavored with fruit juice if desired, rather than rum) as a nibble instead of chips, although they always seem to make an appearance, and as an occasional treat, that's fine. Perhaps it's the idea of seeing myself in a bathing suit that makes me choose a low-fat healthful appetizer. Grilled Chicken in Herb Marinade began its soaking the day before and is brought to the picnic in the marinade. When I was growing up, it just wasn't a picnic unless Grandma brought her Cabbage and Shrimp Slaw, and these days, my friends clamor for my Orzo Salad Pistou. In the best summer tradition, Handmade Lemon-Limeade staves off thirst, and can be turned into a daiquiri with a splash of rum. (Rum is a seasonal beverage for me, one that just seems best in warm weather, disregarding the occasional hot buttered rum during the holidays.) For many years, I worked at a test kitchen for a magazine devoted to chocolate, so I can say that chocolate was literally my life. While I still crave deep, dark chocolate, I also love butterscotch blondies, especially Blondies with White Chocolate Chips and Raspberries.

A couple of words of caution about outdoor grilling. As you may be spending all afternoon in the sun, don't forget the sunscreen. Also, no matter how hot it gets, do not cook in your bathing suit. I don't say this to be funny. Always cover up with a short-sleeved shirt, pants, and some kind of shoes. Especially when grilling is concerned, it's safety first.

PREPARATION TIMETABLE

Up to 3 days ahead:
* Make Marinade for Grilled Chicken; cover and refrigerate.

Up to 2 days ahead:
* Make Spiked Yogurt Dip; cover and refrigerate.

Up to 1 day ahead:
* Prepare fruits for dip; cover and refrigerate.
* Marinate Grilled Chicken; cover and refrigerate.
* Make Cabbage and Shrimp Slaw; cover and refrigerate.
* Make Orzo Salad; cover and refrigerate.
* Make Lemon-Limeade; cover and refrigerate.
* Make Blondies with White Chocolate Chips; cover with plastic wrap and store at cool room temperature.

Just before serving:
* Reseason the slaw and orzo salad.

FRESH SUMMER FRUITS WITH SPIKED YOGURT DIP

Makes 2 cups

Yogurt's tangy flavor is a great appetite-teaser, but it thins out when liquid flavorings are added. By draining off the yogurt's whey, you get a thick, cheeselike mixture that can be flavored in many ways. Use whatever fruits are at their peak, but this just-sweet-enough dip is sensational with peaches or melon, and has the added benefit of being low in fat.

1 quart plain low-fat yogurt
⅓ cup honey
2 tablespoons dark rum or thawed apple juice concentrate
Assorted fresh fruits (such as peach or nectarine slices, peeled melon wedges, strawberries, pineapple spears), for dipping

1. The day before serving, place a wire sieve over a deep bowl and line with a double layer of cheesecloth. Place yogurt in sieve and place in refrigerator. Let stand overnight until yogurt is thickened. (You can speed the draining by covering the yogurt with a saucer that fits inside the sieve and weighting the saucer with a heavy can. Let stand at room temperature until excess whey is pressed from yogurt and yogurt is

thickened, about 2 hours.) Discard whey and transfer thickened yogurt to a medium bowl. Stir in honey and rum. Cover and refrigerate until well chilled, at least 2 hours. *The dip can be prepared up to 2 days ahead, covered, and refrigerated.*

2. When ready to serve, transfer dip to a small serving bowl and place on a platter. Surround with fruits for dipping and serve immediately.

GRILLED CHICKEN IN HERB MARINADE

Makes 8 to 12 servings

Marinated chicken is a prime choice for the grill, but it really isn't the easiest thing to cook outdoors. My method guarantees excellent results—no more chicken that is charcoal black on the outside and raw within. The thick, pestolike marinade creates a flavorful crust around the juicy chicken; and by placing the poultry around the cooler edges of the grill, it cooks through without irritating flareups.

2 (3½ pounds each) fryer chickens, cut into 8 pieces each
2 cups packed fresh basil leaves
1 cup packed fresh parsley leaves
⅓ cup chopped fresh oregano, or 1½ tablespoons dried
¼ cup chopped fresh chives, or 1 scallion, chopped
3 tablespoons chopped fresh rosemary leaves, or 1 tablespoon dried
2 large garlic cloves, minced
⅓ cup Dijon mustard
¼ cup fresh lemon juice
¼ cup dry vermouth
½ teaspoon salt
¼ teaspoon crushed hot red pepper flakes
¼ cup extra-virgin olive oil

1. Rinse chickens and pat dry with paper towels. Place in a large bowl.

2. In a food processor fitted with the metal blade, combine the basil, parsley, oregano, chives, rosemary,

and garlic; pulse to chop. Add mustard, lemon juice, vermouth, salt, and red pepper flakes. With the machine running, slowly pour oil through feed tube until marinade is smooth. You can also combine all of the ingredients in a blender, in batches, and run until smooth. *The marinade can be prepared up to 3 days ahead, covered, and refrigerated.* Add to chicken and mix well until coated. Cover with plastic wrap and refrigerate at least 4 hours or overnight.

3. Build a hot fire in a charcoal grill. Lightly oil the grill rack. Grill chicken in center area of grill, skin side down, turning once, until barely beginning to brown, about 5 minutes. Arrange chicken in a circle around outside edges of grill. Cover with grill lid (or fashion a dome out of a double thickness of heavy-duty aluminum foil) and cook, turning once, until the juices run clear yellow when pierced with the tip of a sharp knife, about 45 minutes. (If using a gas grill, preheat one side of grill. Adjust heat to medium, then place chicken on non-preheated area of grill. Cook, turning occasionally, until cooked through, about 45 minutes.)

CABBAGE AND SHRIMP SLAW

Makes 8 servings

When I was growing up in California, my grandmother often made this salad for backyard barbecues. (She sometimes used thickly shredded iceberg lettuce instead of cabbage, and if you choose to do so, don't chill the salad for more than two hours before serving.) It has always been high on my list of favored slaws and is substantial enough to make a terrific light lunch entrée.

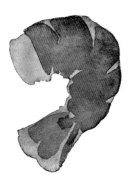

12 ounces medium unshelled shrimp
1 cup mayonnaise
2 tablespoons sherry vinegar, plus additional for reseasoning
1 tablespoon grated onion
½ teaspoon celery seed
¼ teaspoon salt, plus additional for reseasoning
¼ teaspoon freshly ground pepper, plus additional for reseasoning
1 small (1 pound, 4 ounces) head green cabbage, cored and finely shredded (about 8 cups)
4 ripe plum tomatoes, seeded and cut into ½-inch pieces

1. Bring a medium saucepan of lightly salted water to a boil over high heat. Add shrimp and cook until just pink and firm, about 3 minutes. Drain, rinse under cold running water until cool, and drain again. Peel and devein.

2. In a medium bowl, whisk mayonnaise, vinegar, onion, celery seed, salt, and pepper until smooth. Add cabbage, tomatoes, and shrimp. Toss well until combined. Cover and refrigerate for at least 2 hours. *The salad can be prepared up to 1 day ahead, covered, and refrigerated.*

3. Just before serving, reseason with additional vinegar, salt, and pepper. Serve chilled.

ORZO SALAD PISTOU

Makes 8 servings

The culinary term *pistou* refers to two Provençal specialties. One is a luscious basil, cheese, and olive oil puree very similar to the Italian *pesto*. When this heady sauce is stirred into a chunky vegetable soup (often bolstered with pasta), the soup itself is called *pistou*. Here, pasta salad is

given the pistou treatment, creating a refreshing salad with a colorful assortment of verdant green colors. Orzo, a rice-shaped pasta, is easily found at Italian grocers. You may substitute small elbow macaroni or ditali, a short tube-shaped pasta.

8 ounces orzo (rice-shaped pasta)
1 medium zucchini, scrubbed and cut into
   ½-inch pieces
6 ounces green beans, trimmed and cut into
   ½-inch lengths
1 cup fresh or frozen tiny peas
4 scallions, finely chopped
1 cup packed fresh basil leaves
3 tablespoons red wine vinegar
1 large garlic clove, crushed
½ teaspoon salt
¼ teaspoon crushed hot red pepper flakes
¾ cup olive oil
½ cup (2 ounces) freshly grated imported
   Parmesan cheese

1. In a large pot of boiling, lightly salted water, cook pasta until barely tender, about 9 minutes. Drain, rinse under cold water, and drain well. Transfer to a large bowl.

2. Meanwhile, in a medium saucepan of boiling, lightly salted water, cook zucchini just until color is set, about 1 minute. Using a wire sieve or a skimmer, scoop out zucchini and transfer to a large bowl of ice water. Add green beans to the boiling water and cook just until crisp-tender, about 3 minutes. Scoop out and transfer to ice water. Add the peas to the pot and cook just until tender, about 2 minutes for fresh, or 1 minute for frozen. Drain peas, and add to ice water. Drain vegetables well and add to pasta, along with the scallions.

3. In a food processor or blender, combine basil, vinegar, garlic, salt, and hot red pepper. With machine running, gradually add oil and process until smooth. Pour half the dressing over the salad and toss well. Transfer the remaining dressing to a small bowl. Cover salad and dressing separately and refrigerate for at least 2 hours. *The salad and dressing can be prepared up to 1 day ahead, covered, and refrigerated.*

4. When ready to serve, pour the remaining dressing over the salad, sprinkle with Parmesan cheese, and toss well. Serve chilled or at room temperature.

HANDMADE LEMON-LIMEADE

Makes about 3 quarts, 10 to 12 servings

Nothing beats homemade, fresh lemonade as a thirst quencher on a hot summer's afternoon, except maybe this refreshing libation, which also includes fragrant limes in the mix. Add a splash of rum to your drink to make the best daiquiris imaginable.

1 cup fresh lemon juice, including the seeds
1 cup fresh lime juice
1½ cups sugar
2 quarts ice-cold water
Approximately 1 pint light or amber rum (optional)

1. In a blender, blend the lemon and lime juices with their seeds and the sugar until the sugar is dissolved. Strain into a bowl to remove seeds. Divide strained mixture into 2 large pitchers. Stir 1 quart of cold water into each pitcher. Cover and refrigerate until well chilled, at least 2 hours. *The lemon-limeade can be prepared up to 1 day ahead, covered, and refrigerated.*

2. To transport, pour into 2 large thermoses. Pour lemon-limeade into tall glasses over ice, allowing each guest to add rum to taste, if they wish.

BLONDIES WITH WHITE CHOCOLATE CHIPS AND RASPBERRIES

Makes 20 blondies

These chewy butterscotch bars are very adaptable to the baker's whims. Try these with blueberries instead of raspberries, or semisweet chips for the white (but not blueberries and semisweet chips!). Check out my method of lining the baking pan with foil so the blondies can be lifted out in one solid piece for easy cutting (no more ruining the first blondies out of the pan by overzealous digging).

2 cups all-purpose flour
1 teaspoon baking powder
1 teaspoon salt
¼ teaspoon baking soda
10 tablespoons (1¼ sticks) unsalted butter, at room temperature
2 cups packed light brown sugar
2 large eggs, at room temperature
2 teaspoons vanilla extract
1 cup (6 ounces) white chocolate chips
1 cup (6 ounces) fresh raspberries

1. Position the rack in center of the oven and preheat to 350°F. Line a 9-by-13-inch baking pan with a double thickness of aluminum foil so foil extends beyond the 2 opposite short ends of the pan. Fold excess foil down to make handles. Lightly butter and flour inside of foil-lined pan, tapping out excess flour.

2. Sift flour, baking powder, salt, and baking soda onto a large sheet

of waxed paper. In a medium bowl, using a handheld electric mixer set at high speed, beat butter and brown sugar until light in color, about 2 minutes. One at a time, beat in eggs, beating well after each addition. Beat in vanilla. Using a wooden spoon, stir in flour mixture just until smooth. Stir in white chocolate chips. Spread evenly in prepared pan, smoothing top. Sprinkle raspberries over batter.

3. Bake until a toothpick inserted in center comes out with a moist crumb, 30 to 35 minutes. Do not overbake. Cool completely in pan on a wire cake rack.

4. Run a knife around edges of pan to release blondies from sides, being careful not to cut through the foil. Lift up on handles to remove blondies from pan. With a sharp

knife, cut into 20 rectangles, about 2¼ by 3¼ inches each. *The blondies can be prepared up to 1 day ahead, cooled, wrapped individually in plastic wrap, and stored at room temperature. Or cut the blondies into rectangles, cutting down to, but not through, the foil lining. Lift up the blondies on the foil and transfer back to the pan. Cover the entire pan tightly with plastic wrap to store for up to 1 day. For longer storage, refrigerate the blondies, as the fresh raspberries will not keep longer than 1 day at room temperature.*